PRAYING 101

for

PARENTS

By

Dottie Randazzo

Praying 101

for

PARENTS

by

Dottie Randazzo

Creative Dreaming
6433 Topanga Cyn. Blvd.
120
Woodland Hills, CA 91303

ISBN 978-0-6151-5487-9

Prayer does not change God, but changes him who prays.

Soren Kierkegaard

By Dottie Randazzo

Praying 101 for Spiritual Enlightenment

Praying 101 for Kids & Teens

Praying 101 for Men

Praying 101 for Women

Praying 101 for Parents

Introduction

This book is designed for parents because your children can't be watched and protected by you all of the time. Praying adds insurance for their safety.

I realized a long time ago that most of us think that our prayers are not heard because we aren't getting what we want. But it's not that our prayers aren't heard; it's all in the asking. A few years ago, when a friend told me that he wanted something. I asked him if he'd said a prayer for it. He told me he didn't know how to pray.

As a child I attended both Baptist and Lutheran schools where I was taught how to memorize a few really good prayers, such as the Lord's Prayer. I was never really taught how to pray.

I know how to pray. I am not sure how I learned, but I did. All you have to do is ask my sister and she will tell you. She has often said I have a direct line to the heavens!

This book will teach you how to pray. It is your basic prayer book. I have designed a prayer for many aspects of your life. Once you have learned the key ingredients to praying you will have the tools to customize your own prayers. So let's flip the page and begin to solve the mystery of prayer.

Commonly Asked Questions

Do I need to know any special language to pray?

You do not need to know any special language. Your language and words will be understood.

Who do I pray to?

It does not matter whether you are praying to God. Our Father, The Masters of the Universe, or whomever, your prayer will be heard. Pray to the One that you believe in.

When and where should I pray?

Praying can be done anytime and anywhere. If you want to say your prayer in the morning, then that is when you should say it. If you want to say your prayer while standing in line at the supermarket, then that's when you should.

Do I have to kneel down or say my prayer out loud?

No kneeling needed. You can stand, lie down or be sitting in a park. It doesn't matter; your prayer will be heard. Your prayer does not need to be said out loud.

How do I pray?

To pray you use the little voice in your head. The same one that you hear when someone walks into the room with a weird hairdo and you hear in your head, *what was he thinking with that hair?* That's the same voice that you are going to say your prayer with. Those same voices in your head that you hear say, *You did well* or *You should not have done that.* It is almost like talking to yourself except you do it in your head. Say your prayer just like you are writing a letter; begin with "Dear_____." And always end your prayer with thanks. Thanks for listening, thanks for caring, thanks for looking out for me. Gratitude goes a long way in life.

If I don't get what I am asking for, does that mean my prayer was not heard?

Not getting what you want absolutely does not mean that your prayer was not heard. We always get what we want. We may not get it when we want it. We get it when we are supposed to.

In prayer we have the courage, perhaps even the presumption and the arrogance or the audacity, to claim that God's love can be operative in the very specific situations of human need that we encounter.

John E. Biersdorf

Very Important Things
You Should Know

Everything happens for a reason. . If something bad happens to you, you need to look at the experience and see what you were supposed to learn from it. For example, you wanted your child to get accepted into a certain school and he/she didn't. You are upset and angry, this is what you wanted, this is what you planned. Your child then attends a different school, of your choice, and later you learn that the school your child actually attended was better for your child than the school you originally had in mind. Let me remind you that you never know why something happened until the end, when it is all played out. Only after the fat lady has sung and you take the time to look back and reflect. A lot can be said about learning to understand that everything does happen for a reason.

Everything happens exactly when it is supposed to. This might not be when you want it to happen. For example, you want your child to be in the school band and he/she tries out for the band and is not accepted. The following year your child tries out again for the school band and is accepted. When you look back you may notice that it was better that your child was not accepted the first time. Band practice may have taken time away from important studies that first year.

You are doing in your life exactly what you are supposed to be doing at this exact moment. Every single moment in your life is very important and every single moment in your life affects the next moment in your life. Every person that you meet has a reason to be in your life, even if just for a brief moment. Some people come into our lives for a reason and some for a season.

Enjoy your life. You must learn to enjoy your life. Every day that you spend with your child is a day that cannot be duplicated or replaced. Although there may be many more days ahead, each one is different and unique. Each one is a gift. Learn to appreciate every moment and don't take them for granted.

Pray for wisdom. Wisdom is smarts, answers, solutions and brainpower. When you ask for wisdom you ask to be aware of the right answers. Wisdom allows you to see answers when they enter your life. For example, your child wants to go to summer camp and you aren't sure that it's the right thing. You can't come up with a good reason for he/she not to attend camp and you can't think of a good reason for them to attend camp. Pray for a sign that will let you know the right decision to make. If you aren't very good at seeing signs, you can ask for a really big sign as to what your decision should be. Your child may win a scholarship to camp and that would certainly answer your question. An opportunity for your child to do something else during the summer may present itself.

Some-times we get answers but they don't always come to us the way we think that they should and therefore we don't see the answer. We miss them because we are looking for them to be delivered our way. Answers are delivered the way that they are supposed to be delivered, not necessarily the way that we want them delivered.

Believe that your prayers are heard and will be answered. Why pray if you don't have any faith. The bible says that faith the size of a mustard seed can move a mountain. Like Wow! Have you ever seen a mustard seed? It's tiny. Don't try praying to test the system. It doesn't work. The system does not need to be tested by you.

Prayer for Picking the Right School or Day Care for Your Child

Dear Lord,

I pray for the wisdom to make the correct choices regarding the schooling of my child. I pray for the safety of my child. I pray for the wisdom to provide the best possible life for my child complete with a world of opportunities available to him. I pray for the wisdom, strength and courage to take the necessary steps to insure a wonderful life for my child. Thank you for blessing me.

Prayer for a Special Thing for Your Child

Dear God,

My child really wants this special thing. I pray for the wisdom to obtain it. If it isn't meant for him/her to have, I pray for us to have the wisdom to understand why. Thank you for listening to me.

Prayer for Your Child to Get Better Grades in School

Dear Masters of the Universe,

I pray for my child to have the wisdom to obtain better grades. I pray for my child to have the wisdom to have better concentration, better memory and fewer distractions when studying. I pray that you remove any feelings of insecurity that he/she may possess. Thank you for taking care of us.

Prayer for a Pet with Behavioral Problems

Dear Lord,

I pray for the wisdom to be aware of the ways in which I can assist my pet with his/her behavior problems. I pray for the wisdom to see the lessons that are to be learned by this experience. Thank you for blessing us.

Prayer for Your Child's Friendships

Dear Goddess,

I pray for my child to have the wisdom to learn the value of friendships. I pray for my child to have the wisdom to learn that to have a friend, they must be a friend. I pray for my child to have the wisdom to recognize true friends from enemies. I pray for my child to have the wisdom to stand up for themselves and not to be bullied into a bad situation just to fit in. I pray that my child has the wisdom to see and make smart choices. I pray that you protect them from all evil. I pray that you remove any feelings of insecurity that he/she possesses. Thank you for caring about us.

Prayer for Your Child to Resolve Conflicts

Dear Higher Power,

I pray for my child to have the wisdom to make the right choices necessary to resolve the present conflict. I pray for my child to have the wisdom to see the lesson in this situation and that they will be able to grow from it in a positive way. I pray for the wisdom to give them strength and courage to help them resolve the present conflict. I pray that you remove any feelings of insecurity that he/she possesses. Thank you for listening to me.

Prayer for Parents & Children to Understand Each Other Better

Dear Father,

I pray for the wisdom to understand why my children treat me the way that they do. I pray for the wisdom to understand why I treat them the way that I do. I pray for the wisdom to resolve conflicts and add more love into our relationship. I pray for us to have the wisdom to be able to see the lesson in this situation so that we are able to grow from it in a positive way. I pray that you remove any feelings of insecurity that we possess. Thank you for taking care of us.

Prayer for Your Child's Pimples

Dear Lord,

I pray for the wisdom to show me the way to clear up my child's skin. I pray that you will give my child the strength and courage to overcome any humiliation that he/she may feel. I pray that others will not judge him/her because of their skin and that they will be seen for the great person that they are on the inside. I pray for us to have the wisdom to be able to see the lesson in this situation and that we grow from it in a positive way. I pray for the wisdom to each my child to love his/her body. I pray for the wisdom to teach my child that his/her body is a reflection of your creation and it is perfect in every way. I pray that you remove any feelings of insecurity that he/she possesses. Thank you for listening to me.

Prayer for Your Child
to be Loved

Dear God,

I pray for my child to be blessed with
unconditional love. I pray for my child to have
the wisdom to love others unconditionally.
Thank you for taking care of us.

Prayer for the Gift of Time

Dear Masters of the Universe,

I pray for the wisdom to learn to have fun with myself. I pray that you remove any frivolous or too self-indulgent feelings that I may possess about enjoying the life that you have so graciously given me. Thank you for blessing me.

Prayer for Your Child's Eating Disorder

Dear Goddess,

I pray for the wisdom to teach my child to identify bad eating habits from healthy ones. I pray for the wisdom to teach my child strength and courage to make the correct decisions regarding their weight. I pray that others will not judge them because of their weight and that they will be seen for the great person that they are on the inside. I pray for us to have the wisdom to be able to see the lesson in this situation and grow from it in a positive way. I pray for the wisdom to teach my child to love their body. I pray for the wisdom to teach my child that their body is a reflection of your creation and it is perfect in every way. I pray for good health for my child. I pray that you remove any feelings of insecurity that he/she possesses. Thank you for taking care of us.

Prayer for Your Child to Have Good Judgment

Dear Higher Power,

I pray for my child to have the wisdom to make the correct choices and to exercise good judgment in every area of his/her life. Thank you for blessing us.

Prayer for a
Child Who Wears Glasses

Dear Father,

I pray for better eyesight for my child. I pray for the wisdom to teach my child strength and courage to overcome any humiliation that he/she may feel by wearing glasses. I pray that others will not judge him/her because they wear glasses and that they will be see him/her for the great person that they are on the inside. I pray for us to have the wisdom to be able to see the lesson in this situation and grow from it in a positive way. I pray for the wisdom to teach my child to love his/her body. I pray for the wisdom to teach my child that his/her body is a reflection of your creation and it is perfect in every way. I pray that you will remove any feelings of insecurity that he/she possesses. Thank you for taking care of us.

Prayer for a Child to Have Good Health

Dear Lord,

I pray for the wisdom to make the correct choices regarding my child's health and safety. Thank you for taking care of us.

Prayer for a Child Pregnancy

Dear God,

I pray for the wisdom to make the best decisions for my child. I pray for my child's health and the health of my child's baby. I pray for my child to have the strength and courage to stand up for his/her beliefs and themselves. I pray my child has the courage not to be bullied into a bad situation just to fit in. I pray that we have the wisdom to be able to see the lesson in this situation and grow from it in a positive way. I pray that you remove any feelings of insecurity that he/she possesses. Thank you for listening to me.

Prayer for a Missing Child

Dear Masters of the Universe,

I pray that you will guide and protect my child from harm. I pray for the wisdom, strength, and courage to do whatever I need to do to bring my child home safely. I pray for my child to have the wisdom, strength and courage to be safe. I pray that you will bless and protect everyone that is helping to find my child. Thank you for taking care of us.

Prayer for a Child that Wears Braces

Dear Goddess,

I pray for the wisdom to teach my child to have strength and courage to overcome any humiliation that he/she may feel by wearing braces. I pray that others will not judge him/her because of their braces and that they will see him/her for the great person that they are on the inside. I pray for us to have the wisdom to be able to see the lesson in this situation and grow from it in a positive way. I pray for the wisdom to teach my child to love his/her body. I pray for the wisdom to teach my child that his/her body is a reflection of your creation and it is perfect in every way. I pray that you remove any feelings of insecurity that he/she possesses. Thank you for looking out for us.

Prayer for Your Child to Resist Peer Pressures

(Drugs, Sex and Social Pressures)

Dear Higher Power,

I pray for the wisdom to teach my child to make the correct choices. I pray that they have the courage to just say no. I pray for my child to have the strength and courage to stand up for his/her beliefs and themselves. I pray my child has the courage not to be bullied into a bad situation just to fit in. I pray for my child's safety and the safety of others. I pray for my child to have the wisdom to be able to see the lesson in this situation and to grow from it in a positive way. I pray that you remove any feelings of insecurity that he/she possesses. Thank you for taking care of us.

Prayer for Your Child to Have Mental Strength and Courage

Dear Father,

I pray for my child to have mental strength and courage. I pray for my child to have the wisdom to make the correct choices and to stand up for his/her beliefs. I pray my child has the courage not to be bullied into a bad situation just to fit in. I pray that you remove any feelings of insecurity that he/she possesses. Thank you for looking out for us..

Prayer for Your Child's Feelings of Loneliness

Dear Lord,

I pray for us to have the wisdom and strength to remove the loneliness that my child feels inside. I pray that you will send someone into his/her life to have fun with. I pray for us to have the wisdom to be able to see the lesson in this situation and grow form it in a positive way. I pray for my child's awareness that his/her body is a reflection of your creation and it is perfect in every way. I pray that you remove any feelings of insecurity that he/she possesses. Thank you for blessing us.

Prayer for Your Child's Safety in Travels or Vacations

Dear God,

I pray for us to have the wisdom to make the correct choices regarding my child's safety and the safety of others while traveling and/or on vacation. Thank you for taking care of us.

Prayer for Wisdom Regarding Your Child's Sexuality

Dear Masters of the Universe,

I pray for us to have the wisdom to see and make the correct choices regarding my child's sexuality. I pray for us to have the strength and courage to stand up for our beliefs and not to be bullied into a bad situation just to fit in. I pray that others will see my child for the person that he/she is on the inside and not judge them by their sexual preferences. I pray for my child to have the wisdom to love his/her body. I pray that you protect my child from evil. I pray for my child to have the awareness that his/her body is a reflection of your creation and it is perfect in every way. I pray that you remove any feelings of insecurity that he/she possesses. Thank you for looking out for us.

Prayer for Your Child's Happiness

Dear Goddess,

I pray that you will bless my child and those around my child with an abundance of happiness. Thank you for taking care of us.

Prayer for Your Child's Peace and Contentment without Worry

Dear Higher Power,

I pray that you will bless my child with peace and contentment. I pray for my child to have the wisdom to remove all worry from his/her soul. I pray for my child to have the strength and courage to recognize contentment without worry. I pray that you will remove any feelings of insecurity that he/she possesses. Thank you for listening to me.

Prayer for Your Child's Self-Esteem and Self-Worth

Dear Father,

I pray that you bless my child with an abundance of self-esteem and self-worth. I pray for my child to have the wisdom to be able to distinguish self-destructive behavior from productive, healthy behavior. I pray that my child never forgets his/her self-worth. I pray for my child to have the strength and courage to stand up for his/her beliefs and not to be bullied into a bad situation just to fit in. I pray for my child to have the wisdom to love his/her body. I pray for my child to have awareness that his/her body is a reflection of your creation and it is perfect in every way. I pray that you remove any feelings of insecurity that he/she possesses.. Thank you for listening to me.

Prayer for a Child that is Being Bullied

Dear Lord,

I pray for my child to have the courage to stand up for his/her beliefs and not to be bullied into a bad situation just to fit in. I pray that you will remove any fear or anxiety from my child. I pray that you will protect my child from all harm and evil people. I pray for my child to have the wisdom to be able to forgive this person who has bullied them. I pray that my child understands that hate and resentment are not positive. I pray for my child to have the wisdom to remove any hate or resentment he/she may be experiencing. I pray for us to have the wisdom to be able to see the lesson in this situation and to grow from it in a positive way. I pray that you remove any feelings of insecurity that he/she possesses. Thank you for looking out for us.

Prayer for Your Child to Pass a Test

Dear God,

I pray for my child to have the wisdom to remember all the things that he/she have been taught. I pray for my child to have the wisdom to remove any anxiety or confusion. I pray for my child to have confidence in his/her abilities.

I pray that you remove any feelings of insecurity that he/she possesses. Thank you for taking care of us.

Prayer for a Child to Tell the Truth and Not Lie

Dear Masters of the Universe,

I pray for my child to have the wisdom, strength and courage to tell the truth and not lie. I pray that my child will have the courage to stand up for his/her beliefs and not to be bullied into a bad situation just to fit in. Thank you for listening to me.

Prayer for a Child in an Abusive Relationship

Dear Goddess,

I pray for my child to have the wisdom, strength and courage to find a way out of their abusive relationship. I pray that you bless my child with self-love. I pray for their safety. I pray for them to have the strength and courage to stand up for their beliefs and not to be bullied into a bad situation just to fit in. I pray for them to have the wisdom to see and make smart choices in their life. I pray for them to have the wisdom to be able to see the lesson in this situation and to grow from it in a positive way. I pray for them to have the wisdom to love their body. I pray for my child to have the awareness that his/her body is a reflection of your creation and it is perfect in every way. I pray that you remove any feelings of insecurity that he/she possesses. Thank you for blessing us.

Prayer for Your Child to Overcome Hate and Anxiety

Dear Higher Power,

I pray for my child to have the wisdom, courage and strength to remove the hate that he/she feels for another individual. I pray for my child to have the wisdom to remove all anxiety that he/she is suffering from. I pray for my child to have the wisdom to replace those feelings of hate and anxiety with feelings of compassion and understanding. I pray for my child to have the courage to stand up for his/her beliefs and not to be bullied into a bad situation just to fit in. I pray for my child to have the wisdom to be able to see the lesson in this situation and grow from it in a positive way. I pray that you remove any feelings of insecurity that he/she possesses. Thank you for taking care of us.

Prayer for Child's Addictions

(Gambling, Anorexia, Bulimia, Drugs, Alcohol, Smoking, Shopping)

Dear Father,

I pray for us to have the wisdom, strength and courage to recognize things in my child's life that will help him/her overcome their addiction. I pray for my child to have the wisdom to make smart choices and to stand up for his/her beliefs. I pray my child has the courage not to be bullied into a bad situation just to fit in. I pray for us to have the wisdom to be able to see the lesson in this situation and grow from it in a positive way. I pray for my child to have the wisdom to love his/her body. I pray for my child to have the awareness that his/her body is a reflection of your creation and it is perfect in every way. I pray that you remove any feelings of insecurity that he/she possesses. Thank you for listening to me.

Prayer for a Child Suffering from Panic Attacks

Dear Lord,

I pray for my child to have the wisdom, strength and courage to overcome his/her panic attacks. I pray for my child to have the wisdom to be able to see the lesson in this situation and to grow from it in a positive way. I pray for my child to have the wisdom to love his/her body. I pray for my child to have the awareness that his/her body is a reflection of your creation and it is perfect in every way. I pray that you remove any feelings of insecurity that he/she possesses. Thank you for blessing us.

Prayer for Your Child to Forgive Someone

Dear God,

I pray for my child to have the wisdom, strength, courage and compassion to forgive the individual who he/she feels has betrayed them. I pray for my child to have the wisdom to see and make the correct choices in this situation. I pray for my child to have the courage to stand up for his/her beliefs and not to be bullied into a bad situation just to fit in. I pray for my child to have the wisdom to be able to see the lesson in this situation and to grow from it in a positive way. Thank you for blessing us.

Prayer for a Child's Confusion

Dear Masters of the Universe,

My child is confused and does not know what decision is the correct decision. I pray that you bless my child with the wisdom to see and make the correct decision. I pray for my child to have the courage to stand up for his/her beliefs and not to be bullied into a bad situation just to fit in. I pray for my child to have the wisdom to be able to see the lesson in this situation and to grow from it in a positive way. I pray that you remove any feelings of insecurity that he/she possesses. Thank you for looking out for us.

Prayer for Your Child to Be True to Himself/Herself

Dear Goddess,

I pray for my child to have the courage to stand up for his/her beliefs and not to be bullied into a bad situation just to fit in. I pray for my child to have the wisdom to love his/her body. Thank you for looking out for us.

Prayer for a Child Attending a New School

Dear Higher Power,

I pray that you will remove any fear of anxiety from my child about attending a new school. I pray that you will protect them from all harm and evil people. I pray for my child to have the wisdom to make friends and see enemies. I pray for my child to have the courage to stand up for his/her beliefs and not to be bullied into a bad situation just to fit in. I pray for my child to have the wisdom to love his/her body. I pray for my child to have the awareness that his/her body is a reflection of your creation and it is perfect in every way. I pray for my child to have the wisdom to learn what is being taught to them. I pray that you remove any feelings of insecurity that he/she possesses. Thank you for listening to me.

Prayer for a Child's Creativity

Dear Father,

I pray for my child to be abundantly creative on his/her project. I pray for my child to have the wisdom to recognize the creative signs that are being shown to him/her. Thank you for taking care of us.

Prayer for Thanksgiving

Dear Lord,

Thank you for your bounty of blessings. I lovingly rejoice and praise the giver of all good. I realize that I have so much to be thankful for and that all I have is all I need. I pray that you bless me with a grateful heart.

Prayer for Finding a Compromise

Dear God,

I pray for the wisdom to be affable. I pray for the wisdom to see the other person's point of view. I pray for the strength and courage to be flexible. I ask that the highest good be achieved for all parties involved. I pray for the wisdom to trust my instincts. I pray for the wisdom strength and courage not to compromise myself. Thank you for looking out for me.

Prayer to Overcome Negative Spending Habits

Dear Masters of the Universe,

I pray for the wisdom and strength to correct my spending habits. I pray for the strength and courage to leave my credit cards at home and only to use them in extreme emergencies. I pray for the wisdom to make wise choices about saving money instead of spending it. I pray that you remove any feelings of guilt that I may possess regarding my bad choices in the past. I pray for the wisdom to make better choices in the future. Thank you for taking care of me.

Prayer for Reordering Priorities

Dear Goddess,

I pray for the wisdom, strength, courage, peace of mind and clarity to acknowledge, recognize and reorder my priorities so that they can give purpose to my day. I pray for the strength to remember that priorities are not written in granite. I pray for the wisdom and courage to be flexible and change. Thank you for listening to me.

Prayer to Be a Hero

Dear Higher Power,

I pray for the wisdom, strength and courage to be a hero to my children. I pray for the wisdom, strength and courage to keep them protected. I pray for the wisdom to teach them right from wrong. I pray for the wisdom to teach them ethics and integrity. Thank you for listening to me.

Prayer for a Gifted Child

Dear Father,

I thank you for this special child that you have blessed me with. I pray for the wisdom to make my child feel loved and accepted. I pray for the wisdom to let my child know that their gift is a blessing. I pray that my child never feels different or like an outsider. Thank you for listening to me.

Prayer for Sons & Daughters

Dear Lord,

I pray for the wisdom, strength and courage to let my son(s)/daughter(s) live their own life. I pray for the wisdom, strength and courage to not vicariously live through their lives. I pray for the wisdom, strength and courage to offer advice when it is asked for. I pray for the wisdom, strength and courage to let them make their own choices, even if I don't agree. I pray for the wisdom to be reminded that they will learn through their own mistakes. I pray that you will guide and protect them. Thank you for listening to me.

Prayer for a Child Attending a Prom

Dear God,

I pray that my child is directed to be asked or to ask the right person to attend the prom. I pray for my child's safety and the safety of my child's friends at the prom. I pray for the wisdom to teach my child hold to make smart choices on prom night. I pray for the wisdom to be able to teach my child to identify bad choices. I pray for the wisdom to teach my child courage and strength and to stand up for their beliefs and themselves. I pray that my child has the courage not to be bullied into a bad situation just to fit in. I pray that they have a great time and create wonderful memories. I pray that you remove any feelings of insecurity that he/she possesses. Thank you for looking out for us.

Prayer for a New Baby

Dear Masters of the Universe,

I thank you for this baby. I pray for the wisdom, strength and courage to protect and care for my baby. I pray that I will be guided to make the right decisions for me and my baby. I pray that you will bless and protect my baby. Thank you for listening to me.

Prayer to Resolve a Custody Battle

Dear Goddess,

I pray for the wisdom, strength and courage to release this situation to you. I pray for the strength and courage to accept your decision. I pray that you will protect and guide my child. I pray for the wisdom, strength and courage to do what is best for my child and everyone involved. Thank you for listening to me.

Prayer for an Abused Child

Dear Higher Power,

I pray that you heal my child. I pray for the wisdom, strength and courage to heal from this ordeal. I pray that you will bless me and my child with the wisdom so that we can stay protected and prevent this event from occurring again. I pray for my child and I to have the wisdom, strength and courage to forgive and move forward in our lives in a positive way. Thank you for taking care of us.

Prayer for a Child with Special Needs

Dear Father,

Thank you for blessing us with this beautiful child. I pray for the strength and wisdom to guide our child in the right direction(s) regarding his/her special needs. I pray for the wisdom to see the right opportunities that are presented to us. I pray for my child to have the wisdom to love his/her body. I pray for my child to have the awareness that his/her body is a reflection of your creation and it is perfect in every way. I pray that my family has the wisdom to learn what is being taught to them. I pray that you remove any feelings of insecurity that we possess. Thank you for loving us.

Prayer for a Teen Getting his/her Driver's License

Dear Lord,

I pray for the protection of my teenage child. I pray that my child has the wisdom to make smart choices. I pray for the safety of my child and the safety of others. Thank you for looking out for us.

Prayer for a Teen Dating

Dear God,

I pray for the safety of my teen while dating. I pray that he/she be blessed with the wisdom to make smart choices. I pray that he/she has the courage to stand up for his/her beliefs and not to be bullied into a bad situation just to fit in. Thank you for listening to me.

Prayer for Everyday Safety

Dear Masters of the Universe,

I pray for the safety of my family. I pray that you bless us with the wisdom that will keep us protected. I pray that you bless us with the courage to make smart choices for our safety. Thank you for taking care of us.

Prayer to Find a New Home

Dear Goddess,

I pray for the wisdom to be aware of the opportunities to find a new home. I pray for the strength and courage to stand up for myself and my beliefs and not to be bullied into a situation just to fit in. I pray that you remove any insecurity that I may possess. Thank you for blessing me.

Prayer for a Child's Safety on the Internet

Dear Higher Power,

I pray for my child's safety on the internet. I pray that he/she have the wisdom to be aware of what they can do to be safe. I pray that my child have the strength and courage not to be bullied into a bad situation just to fit in. Thank you for blessing us.

Prayer for a Good Night's Sleep

Dear Father,

I pray that you bless me with a good night's sleep. I pray for the wisdom to be aware of the ways in which I can insure that I will have a good night's sleep. Thank you for listening to me.

Prayer to Be a
Great Parent

Dear Lord,

I pray for the wisdom to be aware of the opportunities for me to be a great parent. I pray for the strength and courage not to be bullied into a bad situation just to fit in. I pray that you remove any insecurity that I may possess. Thank you for listening to me.

Prayer to Give a Child the Freedom to Express Himself/Herself

Dear God,

I pray for the wisdom to be aware of the opportunities for my child to freely express himself/herself. I pray for the strength and courage not to impose my ways and beliefs on my child. Thank you for loving us.

Prayer to Be an Inspiration to Other Parents

Dear Masters of the Universe,

I pray for the wisdom to be aware of the opportunities in which I can be an inspiration to other parents. I pray for the wisdom to be the best parent I can possibly be. Thank you for blessing me.

Prayer to Allow a Child to Choose His/Her Own Path in Life

Dear Goddess,

I pray for the strength and courage to allow my child to choose his/her own path in life. I pray that my child has the wisdom to be aware of the opportunities in which he/she can carve their own path in life. Thank you for listening to me.

Prayer for a Peaceful Home

Dear Higher Power,

I pray that you bless our home. I pray for the wisdom to be aware of the opportunities to make our home a peaceful one. Thank you for loving us.

Prayer to Understand Death

Dear Father,

I pray that you will heal the pain in my family's heart. I pray for the wisdom to understand what is being taught to us. I pray that my family will be able to move forward from this sad event. Thank you for taking care of us.

Prayer to Get Your House in Order

Dear Lord,

I pray for the motivation to keep my house clean and my life in order. I pray for the wisdom to be reminded that my home is a reflection of myself. I pray for the wisdom to respect and care for my home as I respect and care for myself. Thank you for blessing me.

Prayer for a Lost Pet

Dear God,

I pray for the safety of my pet. I pray that you will guide and protect him/her and show them the way back home. Thank you for listening to me.

Prayer to Accept Real Life

Dear Masters of the Universe,

I pray for the wisdom, strength and courage to surrender to my life and accept my circumstances. I realize that before I can change anything I must recognize that this is the way it's meant to be right now. I pray for the wisdom, strength and courage to let you lead and the wisdom, strength and courage to follow. I pray for the strength and courage to rise above my stubborn resistance so that I can actually see what is happening in my life. Thank you for taking care of me.

Prayer for a Child's New Home and Neighborhood

Dear Goddess,

I pray that you will bless my child's new home and neighborhood. I pray for the safety of my child in his/her new home and neighborhood. I pray that you will bless my child with an abundance of happy memories in his/her new home and neighborhood. I pray that you remove any feelings of insecurity that he/she possesses. Thank you for taking care of us.

Prayer for a Child to Get the Message

Dear Higher Power,

I pray for my child to have the wisdom to learn what they are suppose to learn during their time here on earth. I pray that they will be guided and protected as they walk through life. I pray for my child to have the wisdom to see the daily miracles that are so graciously sprinkled in their life. Thank you for listening to me.

Prayer for a Sick or Old Pet

Dear Father,

I pray that you bless my pet. I pray that he/she not suffer if it is your will to take him from this planet. I pray for the wisdom, strength and courage to be strong for my pet. I pray for the wisdom, strength and courage to be able to let go of my pet. I pray that you bless my aching heart and remove the hurt and pain. Thank you for taking care of us.

Prayer for The Good Life

Dear Lord,

I pray for the wisdom to live a life of simplicity; free from anxiety. I pray for the wisdom to see and opportunity to be useful and live harmoniously. I pray for the wisdom to remember that housing, food and clothing are what's important. I pray for the wisdom to eliminate the clutter form my life. Thank you for taking care of me.

Prayer to Protect Children

Dear Masters of the Universe,

I pray that you protect my children. I pray that you bless them with the wisdom to be aware of the opportunities to protect themselves. Thank you for taking care of us.

Prayer for Better Learning and Comprehension

Dear Goddess,

I pray for the wisdom to be aware of the opportunities for me to have better learning and comprehension skills. I pray that you remove any insecurity that I may possess. Thank you for blessing me.

Prayer to Have a Great Picnic

Dear Higher Power,

I pray that you will bless us with a great picnic. I pray that we will have the awareness to create great memories. Thank you for loving us.

Prayer for Sharing

Dear Father,

I pray for the wisdom to allow myself to share with others. I pray that I have the courage to share my time, my love, my attention, my knowledge and my material possessions. I pray for the wisdom to know that sharing these things is what makes them so valuable. Thank you for listening to me.

Prayer for Better Communications

Dear Lord,

I pray for the wisdom to be aware of the ways in which I can communicate better. I pray for the strength and courage to stand up for my beliefs and not be bullied into a situation just to fit in. I pray that you remove any insecurity that I may possess. Thank you for listening to me.

Prayer to Overcome Problems at Work

Dear God,

I pray for the wisdom to be aware of the opportunities to overcome my problems at work. I pray for the wisdom to be aware of the lessons for me to learn. I pray that you remove any insecurity that I may possess. Thank you for blessing me.

Prayer for a Child Attending Camp

Dear Masters of the Universe,

I pray for the safety of my child. I pray that my child has the wisdom to learn from this experience. I pray that he/she be blessed with the wisdom to make smart choices. I pray that my child has the wisdom to learn what is being taught to them. Thank you for looking out for us.

Prayer for a Sick/Injured Child

Dear Goddess,

I pray that you will bless and heal my sick and/or injured child. I pray that we are blessed with the patience for my child to heal. I pray for a speedy recovery for my child. I pray that my family has the wisdom to learn what is being taught to them. Thank you for looking out for us.

Prayer for a Child/Teen with Behavioral Problems
(ADD, ADHD, ODD, CD)

Dear Higher Power,

I pray for the wisdom, strength and courage to make the right decisions for my child regarding his/her behavior problems. I ask that you bless us and our family with patience. I pray for my child to have the wisdom to correct his/her behavioral problems. I ask that my child have the wisdom, strength and courage to not be influenced by other children's behavior. Thank you for taking care of us.

Prayer for a Better Job

Dear Father,

I pray for the wisdom to be aware of the opportunities for me to find a better job. I pray for the wisdom to be aware of the lessons for me to learn. I pray that you remove any insecurity that I may possess. Thank you for listening to me.

Prayer for a Child that is Smoking and/or Doing Drugs

Dear Lord,

I pray for my family to have the wisdom, strength and courage to deal with my child's smoking. and/or drug habit(s). I pray for my family to have the patience that is necessary in this situation. I pray that my child be blessed with the wisdom, strength and courage to see that smoking and/or drug use is not in his/her best interest. I pray that my child have the courage to stand up for his/her beliefs and not be bullied into a bad situation just to fit in. Thank you for loving us.

My Personalized Prayers

My Personalized Prayers

PRAYER FOR/TO

.

www.ingramcontent.com/pod-product-compliance
Lightning Source LLC
Chambersburg PA
CBHW032015040426

42448CB00006B/643